George Washington Carver

George Washington Carver

by Andy Carter and Carol Saller
illustrations by Lance Paladino

On My Own
BIOGRAPHY

Carolrhoda Books, Inc./Minneapolis

Text copyright © 2001 by Andy Carter and Carol Saller
Illustrations copyright © 2001 by Lance Paladino

This book is available in two editions:
Library binding by Carolrhoda Books, Inc.,
  a division of Lerner Publishing Group
Soft cover by First Avenue Editions,
  an imprint of Lerner Publishing Group
241 First Avenue North
Minneapolis, MN 55401 U.S.A.

Website address: www.lernerbooks.com

Library of Congress Cataloging-in-Publication Data

Carter, Andy, 1948–
    George Washington Carver / by Andy Carter and Carol Saller ; illustrations by Lance Paladino.
        p.   cm. — (On my own biography)
    Summary: Recounts the life of the African-American agriculturist at the Tuskegee Institute, emphasizing his love of plants and his belief in living in harmony with the natural world.
    ISBN 1-57505-427-2 (lib. bdg. : alk. paper) ISBN 1-57505-458-2 (pbk. : alk. paper)
    I. Title. II. Series. III. Saller, Carol. IV. Paladino, Lance, 1968– ill. 1. Carver, George Washington, 1864?–1943—Juvenile literature. [1. Carver, George Washington, 1864?–1943. 2. Agriculturists. 3. Afro-Americans—Biography.]
    S417.C3 C28   2001
    630'.92—dc21   99-006825

Manufactured in the United States of America
5 6 7 8 9 10 – JR – 09 08 07 06 05 04

To Diane, Ken, and Amanda — A.C.

To Richard, John, and Ben — C.S.

For Mom and Dad — L.P.

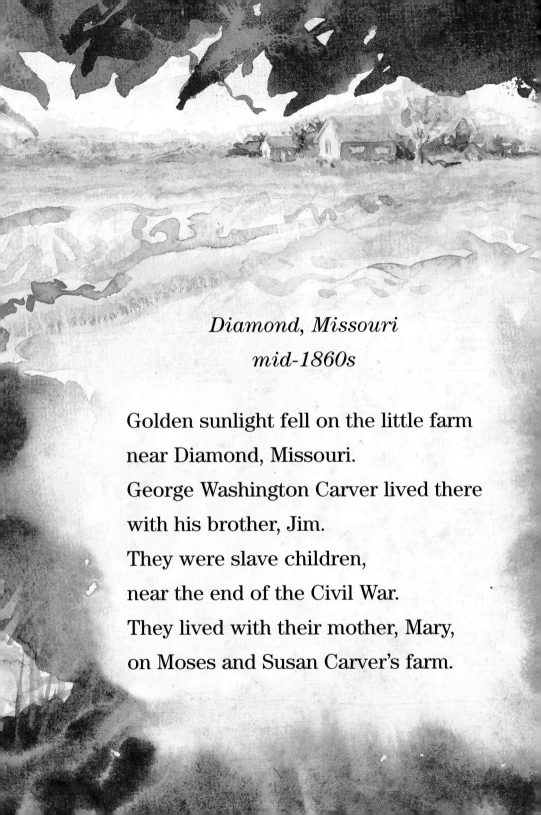

Diamond, Missouri
mid-1860s

Golden sunlight fell on the little farm
near Diamond, Missouri.
George Washington Carver lived there
with his brother, Jim.
They were slave children,
near the end of the Civil War.
They lived with their mother, Mary,
on Moses and Susan Carver's farm.

Many masters mistreated slaves.

But the Carvers were kind people.

When George was just a baby,

he and his mother were stolen

from the Carvers.

Kidnappers planned to sell them

to new masters.

Mary was never found.

But Moses Carver got George back.

The Carvers treated George and Jim

more like their own children

than like slaves.

Even after slavery ended,

George and Jim lived on the farm.

George was small and weak
and often sick.
He was not strong enough for farm work.
So while Jim helped Moses,
George worked around the house
with Susan.
Inside, George swept the dirt floors.
He helped cook on the big stove.
He learned to knit and sew.
Outside, George washed clothes in a tub.
He tended Susan's garden.

When George's chores were done,
he would head for the woods.
George loved to find secret places
in the trees.
He found cool places by the streams.
He found lazy places in the meadows.
Rocks and frogs and crawling things
were his playmates.

George would be gone all day if he could.

He liked roaming and climbing and looking
and wondering.

He found questions everywhere.

What makes a flower grow?

Why does a bird sing?

Is there a name for every insect, bird,
and flower?

George loved the things he found
in the woods.
He wanted to keep them.
Sometimes his pile of rocks would grow
too large to keep in the cabin.
Susan would make
George throw the rocks out.
One by one, George would throw
the rocks down the hill.

But he always saved his favorites,
to start a new pile.

One day, George brought some
milkweed plants into the cabin.
He wanted to study them.
But first he had chores to do.
Susan put the iron in the fire
to make it hot.

George climbed on a chair
and put the plants up high,
out of the way.
George folded the clean, warm clothes
after Susan ironed them.
The cabin grew very warm.

17

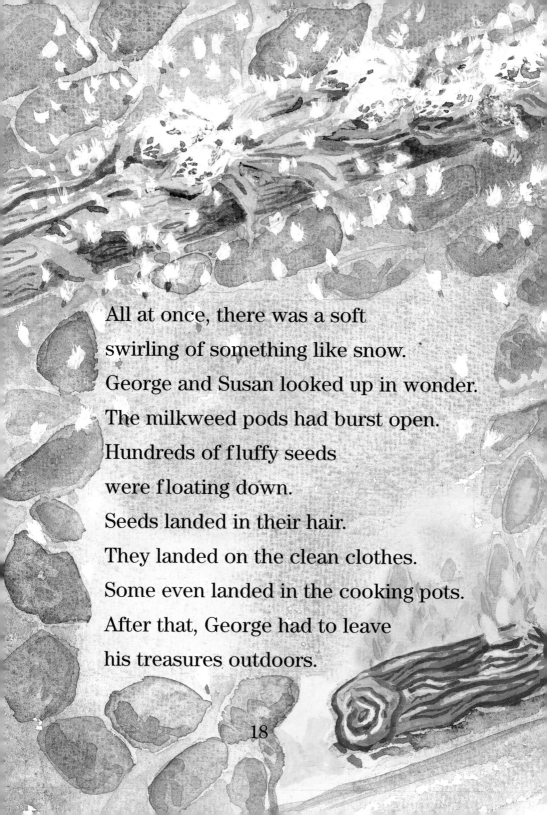

All at once, there was a soft
swirling of something like snow.
George and Susan looked up in wonder.
The milkweed pods had burst open.
Hundreds of fluffy seeds
were floating down.
Seeds landed in their hair.
They landed on the clean clothes.
Some even landed in the cooking pots.
After that, George had to leave
his treasures outdoors.

18

George longed to understand
how living things grew.
He tried to find answers to his questions.
In a small clearing not far from the cabin,
he made his own secret garden.
There he replanted flowers
he found in the woods.

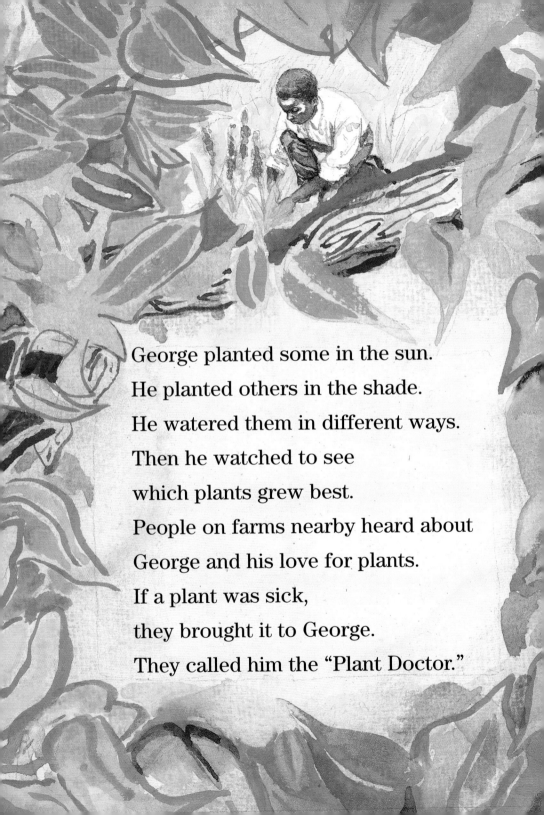

George planted some in the sun.

He planted others in the shade.

He watered them in different ways.

Then he watched to see

which plants grew best.

People on farms nearby heard about

George and his love for plants.

If a plant was sick,

they brought it to George.

They called him the "Plant Doctor."

George had tender feelings
for all his plants.
Once, he was caring for
a plant.
He accidentally broke
some of the roots.
Tears came to his eyes.
He knew the plant would die.

In the woods, George saw how nature
provided food for plants and animals.
Even dead plants were useful.
He saw them turn soft and brown.
And after a while, they broke down
and went back into the soil.
They made food for new plants to grow.
Nature, George saw, did not waste things.

George's discoveries only filled him
with more questions.
He didn't know where
to find the answers.
But he wondered
if he could find them in books.
Moses could not read.
But Susan knew how.
She taught George from a spelling book.
For hours, George sat with the speller.
He learned each and every word.
It was the only book he had.
And it could not answer his questions.
So George began to dream
of going to school.

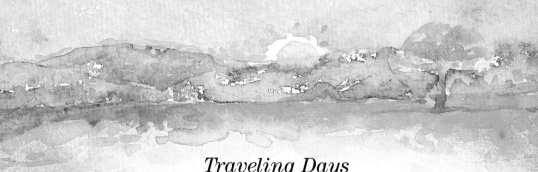

Traveling Days
1870s to 1890s

There was a school not far away.

But it was for white children.

George was not welcome there.

The nearest school for black children

was at Neosho.

That was eight miles away.

It must have seemed a very long way

to a small boy.

But George's yearning to learn

was strong.

George told Moses and Susan

he wanted to go to school.

When he left the Carvers' farm,

George was only 11 years old.

He had no money.

He didn't know anyone in Neosho.

Soon he found a family to live with.

To pay for his room and food,

he worked hard before and after school.

George was happy to go to school.
But before long,
he knew as much as his teacher.
And for George, that was not enough.

George left Neosho in the late 1870s.

For several years, he traveled.

Everywhere he went,

he searched for an education.

George's search was not easy.

Most schools would not accept

black students.

George always had to work hard

to have enough money.

He worked as a cook

when he went to high school in Kansas.

He took in laundry

when he went to college in Iowa.

In high school and college,
George took art classes.
He painted beautiful pictures of plants.
George thought about becoming an artist.

But he decided he could help his people
more by becoming a scientist.
In college,
George discovered ways
to make soil better for plants.
He learned so much at Iowa State College
that his teachers asked him
to be a teacher there.

Tuskegee Years
1896 to 1943

While teaching in Iowa,

George heard about a school in Alabama.

At the Tuskegee Institute,

all the teachers and students were black.

The goal of the school was to help

black people succeed.

Booker T. Washington was

the president of Tuskegee.

He asked George to teach there,

and George said yes.

At Tuskegee, George taught classes.

He also met many farmers.

The farmers worked hard planting cotton.

But the plants did not grow well.

The soil was worn out.

George wanted to use science
to help poor farmers grow better crops.
So he traveled in a wagon to farms.
His wagon was a classroom on wheels.
George showed farmers
how to make their soil healthier.

He showed farm women
how to preserve fruits and vegetables
for the winter.
And he showed them how to use
wild plants to make healthy food
for themselves and their animals.

People also wanted beauty
in their homes.
So George showed them how to make
colorful paints from the soil.
And he gave them flower seeds
for their gardens.

George knew that growing cotton
for many years could hurt the soil.
From his studies in college,
he discovered that growing peanuts
could make it rich again.
George wanted farmers to grow peanuts.
But farmers said nobody would buy them.
So George began to study peanuts.
He knew you could eat them.

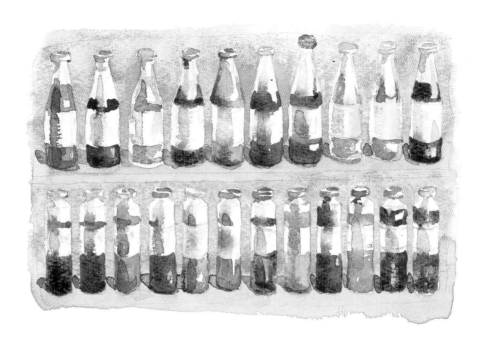

But he wondered,

were there other ways to use them?

He baked them and squeezed them.

He studied the shells and the leaves.

Soon he had made paint, milk,

shaving cream, and shoe polish.

Altogether, he made more than

three hundred things from peanuts!

Once, George and his students
at Tuskegee cooked a big dinner.
They made soup, salad,
and a dish that tasted like chicken.
The people at the dinner were surprised
when George told them
everything was made from peanuts.
George became famous
for his work with peanuts.
He spoke to Congress
and traveled all over the United States.
He won prizes and awards for his work.
People wrote about him in the newspaper.
They called him the "Peanut Man."

George's work with peanuts
was important.
But his ideas about nature
are his most lasting gift.
As a child, George learned that in nature,
there is no waste.

As a man, he taught farmers
to use everything nature gave them.
George helped farmers make
their soil richer and their lives better.
He taught them how to live
in harmony with nature.
During his life, his ideas were new.
People did not understand them.
Like some of the flowers
in his secret garden,
George Washington Carver's ideas
took a long time to bloom.

I am not a finisher... I am a blazer of trails.
Others must take up the various trails of truth,
and carry them on.

George Washington Carver

Afterword

In addition to being a gifted teacher and inventor, George Washington Carver was a skilled artist, musician, and gardener. But in spite of his love for these pursuits, he chose to work as an agricultural scientist. He thought he could help his people the most by helping black farmers keep their farms.

When Carver said "I am a blazer of trails. Others must take up the various trails of truth, and carry them on," he knew that it would be a long time before black people were treated as equals. He knew that poor black farmers had a long struggle ahead of them to save their farms from debt and failure.

The plight of black farmers has not gone away. In 1999, the Black Farmers and Agriculturalists Association marched in Washington, D.C., to protest unfair treatment. They believe the United States government discriminates against black farmers in granting farm loans. Some of the marchers wore T-shirts with a picture of George Washington Carver on the front. The picture served as a reminder that the problems of black farmers are not new. And it was a reminder that others have taken up Carver's "trails of truth" and are carrying them on.

Important Dates

1865?—George Washington Carver is born at Diamond, Missouri. His date of birth and the identity of his father are not known.

1865?—George and his mother, Mary, are kidnapped. Mary never returns, but Moses Carver finds George and brings him back.

1877?—George leaves Diamond for school in Neosho.

1891—George begins studying at the State Agricultural College in Ames, Iowa.

1893—George receives an award for his painting at the World's Columbian Exposition in Chicago.

1894—George earns a bachelor's degree and then joins the teaching faculty at Iowa State College.

1896—George earns a master's degree. He goes to Tuskegee Institute to be Director of Agriculture and begins to help local farmers.

1921—George addresses the U.S. House Ways and Means Committee on the uses of peanuts.

1923—George receives the Spingarn Medal for Distinguished Service to Science.

1943—George dies in Tuskegee, Alabama, on January 5 at about 78 years of age.